MURIEL STEFFY LIPP

Secrets of the Forest

ILLUSTRATED BY MARK COYLE

NORTHWORD
PRESS, INC.

Minocqua, Wisconsin

For Ryan, Jacqueline, and Lawrence

NorthWord Press, Inc.
P.O. Box 1360
Minocqua, WI 54548

Book design by Lisa Moore

ISBN 1-55971-456-5

Library of Congress Cataloging-in-Publication Data
Lipp, Muriel K. Steffy.
    Secrets of the forest / by Muriel Steffy Lipp: illustrations by Mark Coyle.
        p.   cm.
    ISBN 1-55971-456-5 (hardcover)
    1. Forest fauna—Juvenile literature. 2. Wildlife watching—
Juvenile literature. [1. Forest animals. 2. Wildlife watching.]
I. Coyle, Mark, ill. II. Title.
    QL112.L57   1995
    591—dc20   94-47033

Printed in Malaysia

MURIEL STEFFY LIPP

Secrets of the Forest

ILLUSTRATED BY MARK COYLE

Roscoe's family was camping in the woods. Near their tent rushed a clattering creek.

"There are animals by this creek," said Papa.

"Where?" asked Roscoe.

"Under the stones, inside the holes, between the roots, and back in the green, dark woods," said Papa.

Roscoe thought about that. He thought about a thousand animal eyes peeping at him from the green, dark woods.

"I want to see animals," said Roscoe.

"You have to be very, very quiet," said Papa.

"Why?" asked Roscoe.

"Wild animals are afraid of us," said Papa.

"I can be quiet for a long, long time," said Roscoe.

Roscoe showed his father how he could be quiet. He pinched his lips and stood very still. He was quiet for 1, 2, 3, 4, 5, 6, 7, 8, 9, 10.

In all that time, no animals showed themselves to Roscoe.

"No animals," said Roscoe. "Why?"

"That's quiet, but not long enough," said Papa.

Roscoe picked up flat pebbles to skip over the water. Papa skipped pebbles, too.

"I'm going to watch for animals near sundown," said Papa. "I'll watch for half an hour by the creek. Maybe some animals will come by for a drink of water. If you can sit as still as a stone— not a wiggle or a moan—you can watch with me."

"OK," said Roscoe, throwing a pebble.

It was quiet in the woods when Papa and Roscoe sat by the creek. Papa had a notebook so he could write down the animals he saw. Roscoe had a notebook, too.

"Remember," said Papa. "Not a sound! We sit as still as a stone. If you can't sit still, you'll have to go back to camp."

"OK," said Roscoe. But he wondered if he could *ever* sit as still as a stone.

Roscoe and his father and the stones sat very still. A bird dipped in the water upstream. Then it flew off, straight up. Papa wrote: SWALLOW.

Roscoe looked at Papa's notebook. In his own notebook he wrote:
SWALLOW.

As they sat by the creek, Roscoe's foot itched.

Roscoe wrote: MOSKEETO.

Papa smiled. He scratched his arm, then wrote: mosquito.

SWALLOW

SWALLOW

MOSKEETO mosquito

The woods were quiet.
"Shhhhh," the wind whispered.
But the creek was not quiet. Roscoe
thought he heard it sing:

> *Booli-booli bog*
> *frog and log*
> *booli-booli bog*
> *fishes and swishes.*

Just then Roscoe heard a swish.
He turned his head and saw a flash of
silver jump from the water.

Roscoe wrote: FISH.

Papa wrote: trout.

Seeing the trout helped Roscoe sit
still for another two minutes, but it
seemed like ten hours. Where were
the animals?

Roscoe looked at the millions of humpy, bumpy pebbles in the creek. They could sure sit still!

Roscoe thought he would turn into a humpy-bumpy pebble if he sat there any longer. He got up from the rock. He hopped to another rock. His right leg was stiff. It tingled and bubbled like drinking a cold soda.

Roscoe walked back down the path to their camp.

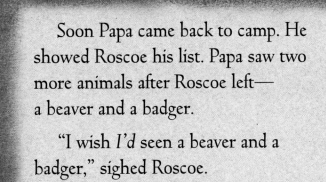

Soon Papa came back to camp. He
showed Roscoe his list. Papa saw two
more animals after Roscoe left—
a beaver and a badger.

"I wish *I'd* seen a beaver and a
badger," sighed Roscoe.

"Maybe tomorrow night," said Papa.

The next day, Roscoe and Papa sat by the creek again.

Suddenly they heard a loud noise behind them. "I WANT TO WATCH ANIMALS, TOO!" said the noisemaker.

The noisemaker was Patty, Roscoe's younger sister.

"Shhhhh!" said Papa. "If you want to watch animals with us, you have to be very quiet."

"OK," said Patty in a loud voice. "I'LL BE VERY QUIET."

"She can't be quiet," said Roscoe to Papa.

"I CAN TOO!" yelled Patty.

"Let's all try," whispered Papa.

Patty ran back to camp to get a notebook so she could write down her animals, too.

"She can't even spell good," grumbled Roscoe to his father.

When Patty came back, she had a big notebook Mama gave her and a purple crayon.

"Patty, find a comfortable rock. Can you sit as still as a stone?" asked Papa.

"YES!" said Patty. "I CAN SIT AS STILL AS A STONE."

Patty and Roscoe and Papa sat very still. So did the rocks and the trees and the roots. Only the creek chattered and clattered, singing and bubbling.

Suddenly, something darted out from the woods. It circled. It swooped and dipped. Roscoe started to print: SWALLOW. Then he looked at Papa's notebook. It said: bat.

Roscoe crossed out his word
and wrote BAT. Roscoe peeped at
Patty's paper. In big purple letters,
it said: BIRD.

Roscoe was tired of sitting. Patty was being very still. He wondered if she was tired of sitting, too.

Suddenly a tree branch moved. Roscoe saw something scamper to the end of the branch. It was a squirrel.

SQUIRL

squirrel

SKQL

Roscoe wrote: SQUIRL.

Papa wrote: **squirrel**.

Patty wrote: SKQL.

Roscoe knew her spelling was wrong.

They watched the squirrel jump to another branch. Then it ran down the tree and disappeared.

Thump! Thump! they heard. What was going on?

Papa, Patty, and Roscoe waited for the thump-thump to show itself.

Nothing.

Patty slipped her feet into the cold water.

Giggle, wiggle, swish,
frogs and logs and fish,
giggle, wiggle, swish.

The water sang to Roscoe. It helped him keep his feet quiet.

The thumping in the woods got louder. And two heads burst out of the leaves along the creek.

Deer! A mother and her baby. They had big, wild eyes. They looked right at Roscoe. He wanted to touch them. It was harder than ever to sit still.

The mother deer sniffed. The small, spotted fawn stood bravely in front. The fawn sniffed, too. Then they turned and thump-thumped back into the green, dark, safe woods.

Roscoe's eyes got wider and wider.
He wrote: 2 DEERS.

Papa smiled.

He wrote: 1 doe 1 fawn.

Patty hugged her knees and giggled.
Roscoe saw her big purple letters:
MOMMY BABY.

"I'm so proud of both of you. You're
the quietest animal watchers I've ever
seen!" said Papa.

Papa put his arm with the notebook
around Roscoe. He put his arm with the
pencil around Patty. Together they
walked bumpily, noisily, happily back to
their camp.

2 DEERS

1 doe 1 fawn

MOMMY BABY